Dear GEW friend,

Thank you for ordering " The Time Manager's Guide to Organising Your Life."

This comprehensive guide provides essential tools for managing time effectively, including two essays on time management, a daily planner and a task list. This book will give readers the skills and knowledge to optimise their time and organise their lives. If so, please consider writing a review. Your feedback would be greatly appreciated! We are committed to customer satisfaction and always look for ways to improve our products and services. Please do not hesitate to contact us with any questions or suggestions.

Thank you again for your purchase. We look forward to hearing from you soon!

Sincerely,

Global East-West (GEW). London.
mail@global-east-west.com
https://global-east-west.com

PUBLISHER

Contents

Remote Employment? The clock is ticking!

I've heard that the freedom to set one's work hours is a major draw of working from home. However, while it's true that telecommuting allows you to establish your own schedule, this does not negate the need for regular work hours.

Working on a 'hit or miss' basis without a set schedule is untenable. The clock is ticking! Time, YOURS!

The benefits of working from home can be enormous. You may see the kids off to school and be there to greet them when they return. While you're busy working, throw a load of laundry into the washing machine and let it go through its cycles.

You'll have plenty of time to prepare dinner before your hungry relatives swarm like vultures. Those are all genuine benefits that come with working from home.

Working from home may be a blessing or a curse depending on how effectively you organise your time and create a routine that works for you and your family. When working from home, every minute counts.

You need to maximise the effectiveness of your working hours. Either you will spend too much time working or you will fail horribly at your work from home job or business if you are inefficient at getting the necessary duties done.

When you work from home, you must establish and stick to a strict work plan for yourself and the people in your immediate circle.

A job in the real world serves two purposes: (1) it gives you something to look forward to each day, and (2) it lets your loved ones know that you have other commitments during the week. Both of these benefits of having a regular job involve using your time.

Let's start with the framework of a traditional job and talk about how you may adapt that to your at-home career or business. When you have a job that requires you to leave the house, you have certain hours and days that you must be there.

The same level of organisation is required when working from home. You must establish regular work hours. The flexibility of a work-from-home career comes with the responsibility of picking your work schedule.

Let's discuss how your loved ones will react to your newfound freedom to work from home. Although you are working and cannot be expected to leave your job to run errands, your darling mother would never call you at your "real" job and ask you to drive Aunt Rosie to the beauty shop and wait for her. Right?

When you're hard at work at home, that caring mother will call to ask you to take Aunt Rosie to the salon so she can get her hair done while you wait. Why? This is because you are present and available at home.

The job you do from home will never be considered "real" by your loving mother. Both you and your partner will appreciate the freedom to run errands. In the eyes of your pals, you are always accessible for lengthy phone chats, lunches, and coffee get-togethers.

The issue is obvious to you. Others will not respect your timetable or routine if you don't do it yourself first. Your time will be consumed unless you treat your work from home like a REAL job with REAL working hours. Then, you won't be able to finish everything that needs doing.

If you don't treat your work-from-home job like the REAL THING with set working hours that keep you from participating in other activities, you'll eventually fail and have to start looking for a REAL job again.
If you want to maximise your time working from home, it's best to create a routine and communicate it to your loved ones.

No need to get disrespectful, but firmness is required. Clear the air for everyone. Monday through Friday, my work hours will be 9 a.m. to 3 p.m. I cannot do personal things like run errands, answer the phone, or host guests on those days and at those times. Keep to your plan!

Time management advice for home-based business owners

For many who run businesses from home, their time is their most precious commodity. Without the passage of time,...time that is extremely valuable!

No matter how many items you have on your "to-do" list or how much money you have, you still only have the standard twenty-four hours in a day. On occasion, an extra twenty-four hours would be welcome, but alas, that will never be the case. I bet you could use some extra time in your day, too.

The problem with our twenty-four-hour days is that we can't possibly fill them all with work. Some of them need to go to sleep tonight. We need to stop every so often to eat, and we even have to take a shower!

Time spent with loved ones is essential. Relationships require care and attention. That being said, we can only put in so many hours every day. We need to maximise the effectiveness of our time in the office because it is finite. We can't afford to dither over trivial matters or delegate work to others.

If you can shave off a few minutes here and there, you'll be able to do more with the time you have. In an effort to respect both of our time, I will be succinct in offering the following advice.

• Effective use of multiple email accounts We all have multiple email accounts. We have a separate account for this and a third for that. If you have many email accounts and find yourself having to check each of them more than once a day, you can save yourself a lot of time by having all of your emails delivered to a single Gmail inbox. Managing many email accounts can be cumbersome, but consolidating them into a single one might save you time and effort.

In addition, you can save time by ignoring emails that won't contribute to your bottom line.

There are many different kinds of email. Emails can be classified as either business-related, non-business-related, or frivolous and time-wasting. Don't bother reading an email that's been forwarded multiple times.

Don't bother with an email that's obviously meant for a large audience. Time spent on email can add up quickly. You should only respond to emails that directly pertain to your business and delete the rest.

• Create schedules to help you stay on track throughout the day: A productive workday is one that goes according to plan. If you plan ahead and can see at a glance what you have to do next, you'll be able to get a lot more done in a shorter amount of time. As a visual learner, I appreciate visual aids. One useful tool is a timetable. It can aid in the effective allocation of your time.

If you want your business to succeed, you need to devote your time and energy to the things that will bring about those results, so keep that in mind when you plan your workday. Don't exert unnecessary effort on things that other people can handle.

Don't rush into outsourcing decisions. When you have people handle the routine aspects of your business, you get back valuable time that you can use elsewhere.

Bookkeeping, accounting, article/E-book writing and submission, trip/event planning, and copywriting are all examples of work that can be contracted out. You should delegate these responsibilities to others so that you may focus on expanding your business, networking, and making sales.

Like I said, spending time with loved ones is important, but you can waste a lot of time doing things like watching television that don't contribute to your goals.

If you keep track of how you spend your time for a few days, you will be astounded at how much of each day goes to waste.

Don't get the wrong idea. In order to function, we must all take breaks. Each of us, mentally as well as physically, needs to unwind. We can't always be focused on work, but we can minimise time spent on distractions.

Time is a scarce and valuable resource. Every second of every day must be utilised to its fullest potential.

How to Get More Done in Less Time Through Outsourcing

Money can be thought of as time spent. As an online business owner, you should always consider how you may most profitably invest your time. For example, dividing your time at work directly impacts your bottom line.

Let's start with the basics and discuss your online business owner responsibilities:

1. Your goal should be to expand your company.
2. Making money-making connections is your responsibility.
3. It is up to you to think of solutions and implement them.
4. It is up to you to seal the transaction.

Those responsibilities sound about right for an internet entrepreneur like you.

Okay! Let's talk about the parts of becoming an internet entrepreneur that are different from your current work. Simply operating a business online does not make you an expert in finance, marketing, or content creation. It would help if you gained credentials to work in the hospitality or tourism industries. You are not a "jack-of-all-trades" just because you opted to start an online business.

Time is of the essence, and it's easy to fritter it away on activities you just aren't skilled at. Yet, you're the brains behind all of this. It is your responsibility to expand your company, and if you put your focus there, you will succeed.

Doing everything yourself, whether you're excellent at it or not, will drain you of the mental and emotional resources necessary to focus on the areas where you have a competitive advantage.

Every company needs to keep track of its daily financial activities, and even the smallest transactions can result in large tax deductions at the end of the year.

You can't just throw everything into a "miscellaneous" folder, and you also can't spend an hour a day on routine bookkeeping tasks. Professional accountants and bookkeepers will only bill you for their time on your books. This is because they typically serve a large clientele.

In other words, if they spend an hour on your files, you will only be charged for that one hour. It would have taken you at least three or four hours to complete the same work, and you're neither a bookkeeper nor an accountant. So make use of an accountant or bookkeeping service!

• Employ a VA (Virtual Assistant): A virtual assistant will free up many hours of your time by handling the struggle of running your online business.

A virtual assistant can read through your inbox and forward the messages that require immediate attention. Entrepreneurs in the online world receive more spam than anyone else. A competent virtual assistant can also fill the role of a travel agent, booking flights and lodgings on your behalf. Use a virtual assistant!

Use article submission services and ghostwriters: No matter your topic, writing articles and E-books is a crucial aspect of any internet marketing strategy. To establish your credibility online, you'll need to have material for your website and submit articles and E-books to banks and repositories where others can use them along with your resource box.

Your ghostwriter will use your signature file with your name and website while posting on your behalf in online forums and blogs. Some ghostwriters will also distribute your articles and eBooks to various online databases. If the ghostwriter you hire doesn't submit articles for you, you can find another service to do so.

Please take advantage of advertising firms, but be clear about what you want them to accomplish for your company before hiring one. PPC advertisement writing can be purchased reasonably, even saving you a lot of time.

You can only devote so much time to building a successful online business because there are only 24 hours a day. The world does not consist solely of business.

Your loved ones do need time and attention from you. This emphasises the importance of prioritising the growth of your business over the mundane, repetitive duties that may consume so much of your time.

Is Outsourcing an Option?

How to Use "Guerrilla" Strategies to Reduce Costs and Outperform the Competition

The "B" word... oh, the horror! The 'B' term I'm referring to is the budgetary one, not the other one. All budgets are predicated on the same incredibly elementary profit-and-loss formula. The bottom line is calculated by subtracting revenue from operating costs.

If you want to enhance your profit, you can either (1) bring in more money or (2) cut costs. Please let me know if you find a way to do both at once.

We could increase the heat and our profits, which would be great. However, increasing revenue is far more challenging than cutting costs to boost a company's bottom line.

The good news is that working from home has some immediate financial benefits. You can save money on gas by taking public transport to and from work. Of course, it would help if you didn't worry about keeping your professional attire current.

You're home, so make a peanut butter and jelly sandwich. These are great ways to save cash, and they come standard with working from home.

But there are other things you can do to cut down on the cost of working from home. Some suggestions for cost-cutting:

First, you should take your time and buy every new piece of software. Most of us who work from home are also avid gamers. We are mad about software...any software. And before you know it, you have more software than you know what to do with.

Second: Don't Overspend on Software. The size of the programmes that assist us in getting our work done varies widely. You may anticipate having a hundred workers by the end of next year, but there's no need to invest in software that can handle that many people just now. When the moment is right, you can always upgrade. You need to be frugal today and get by with only the bare minimum.

Third: Avoid wasting money on pointless forms of promotion. When first starting, many businesses will throw their budgets at pay-per-click (PPC) advertising. Then, they'll pick every available keyword and phrase and leave the PPC ads up around the clock— the inexcusable squandering of precious marketing resources.

You need to understand the data offered by search engines and tailor your ads so that they only show up in the results under strict conditions and at specific times. It's easy to rack up a PPC bill of several thousand dollars in a short time without generating any revenue.

Fourth: Make the most of promotional opportunities that don't cost you a dime. PPC advertising and paid advertising in E-zines and newsletters aren't the only ways to promote your business online; there are free options that can be just as powerful. Free marketing strategies include:

- Create electronic books and articles, and distribute them freely through online book repositories and article banks. (Your name and website address will appear in a resource box at the end of these articles and E-books.)

- The second step is to make relevant blog and forum posts about the goods and services you offer. Your name and URL are in your signature, which you've posted above.

- Another way to spread the word without spending a dime is to exchange banners with a website owner whose offerings complement your own.

- Create a massive opt-in subscriber list. Email marketing is cost-effective, but only if the recipient consents to receive promotional emails.

- Figure out how to make your email promotions go viral. Many strategies exist to get people to forward your promotional emails to their contacts.

Fith suggestion: Get on a reliable long-distance phone provider that has a flat fee. Since the internet is a global marketplace, it is easy to rack up a long-distance bill of several thousand dollars quickly. You can save significant money over time by switching to a flat-rate long-distance telephone plan.

Income minus expenses equal profit, so always keep that in mind.

It's nice to bring in more cash, but cutting costs is possible if you look hard enough. Saving money ultimately means more money in your pocket, leaving your rivals in the dust.

Essay on Time Management

Introduction

In today's fast-paced world, more than 24 hours are needed to complete everything. This is especially true if you are a student with upcoming big examinations or attempting to achieve a deadline for submitting your most recent project. Still, you're bound to have friends and coworkers who appear to breeze through the same responsibilities as you do. Did you ever stop to consider why? They can juggle everything on their plate because they can manage their time effectively. Time is best utilised when planned for and then used under that plan.

People struggle with time management for a variety of reasons:

1. They put things off, which is one of the most common reasons.

2. They may put off doing what they know they should because they perceive no immediate threat to their well-being.

3. They could be wasting their time on meaningless pursuits. This causes individuals to worry excessively about time constraints as deadlines approach.

4. People need help managing their time well because they need a well-defined end objective.

Setting and working towards a goal may be quite motivating. Therefore, it stands to reason that you would prefer to use your time better if you have a plan in mind. Now that you know how most individuals waste their time, you can focus on improving your time management skills. Here are a few suggestions that should help.

How Do You Manage Your Time?

Many folks wonder what the big deal is with time management. So put, you can organise and make the most of your daily time to get more done and achieve your objectives. Of course, this doesn't imply that you should neglect your personal life in favour of your job. On the contrary, it's important to balance your busy schedule with some downtime to recharge.

If you want to get something done well, you need to take breaks. In other words, if you always rush during the day, it may be a sign that you cannot effectively manage your time. The quality of your job will improve if you're in a hurry to get it done, as you'll be less committed and more focused.

Time management is as easy as creating a daily plan that you stick to religiously. Although it appears simple, many of us must remember our original intentions. Time management and making mental plans for the next day may come naturally to us. But we might have forgotten most of our plans by tomorrow's time. As a result, you may keep meaning to accomplish something while ignoring it.

Writing down your goals and the steps you need to take to achieve them will help you get more done.

When planning your daily activities, it's important to factor in how much time you'll need to complete each task. You can then determine if you have scheduled too much work for one day. If that's the case, you need to rearrange your priorities. Prioritise the truly time-sensitive jobs, and leave the rest for another day.

You may keep tabs on your daily progress by referring to the to-do list you made, broken down by time of day. That way, instead of juggling too many balls simultaneously, you may focus on one or two at a time and get more done.

Time Management and Its Impact on Your Life

The gap between a life with and without effective time management is dramatic. Without effectively managing your time, you may find that endless days have passed without you having accomplished anything significant. Without proper time management, you may feel like you've accomplished very little at the end of each day. That is to say; you will not be as efficient as you had hoped. So, if you want to get more done in your life, you must make some changes, including learning to manage your time better.

Planning out your day in advance is just one aspect of time management. To make the most of time management to your advantage, there are a few important considerations to bear in mind.

To make it effective, you must first determine the specific goals you hope to accomplish within a predetermined time frame each day. That is to say, carefully weigh how important certain options are. Prioritise your efforts based on how urgently they must be completed. Furthermore, you need to know how much time you need to spend on each one so you can allot sufficient time for the tasks you set out to complete each day. You can have a set plan to follow if you write down what you want or need to do each day and create a schedule. This will make it simpler for you to follow through on your goals. Of course, you shouldn't strive to fit everything into an unrealistically tight time frame when creating your plan. Failure to do so may leave you dissatisfied with the day's work.

You can get more done if you learn to manage your time well. If this is relevant to your job, your boss will quickly see that you are getting better at meeting deadlines, and because you can organise your time well, you may even be able to submit reports ahead of schedule, which will further impress your boss.

People who are good at managing their time are also known to be more self-disciplined than those who are not, which could lead to a promotion down the road. Your superiors will uphold you as an example that others should strive to imitate.

Good time management will allow you to run your business more efficiently and effectively. As a result, your productivity will increase, and as a result, your business's bottom line will improve.

Successful time management can have a profound effect on your quality of life. It's a crucial aspect of growing as an individual, too. So if you want to increase the satisfaction you get from achieving your daily goals, you should start doing it now.

Helpful Hints for Better Time Management

With age comes the realisation that you have accomplished little substance and have wasted a great deal of time if you cannot effectively manage your time. Whether working in a traditional office or from home, you must learn to manage your time effectively. You have a lot on your plate between your job and your personal life. Therefore, either of them will benefit if you efficiently use your time. However, this will not occur if you follow these suggestions for better time management.

Realise that you have a finite capacity for getting things done in a particular amount of time because you are only human. You can make things easier on yourself by creating a list of daily goals.

One of the first things you should do is figure out what's most important to you. Then, it's up to you to determine what needs immediate attention and what can wait. Prioritise the tasks that need to be completed quickly. When you've finished the more pressing things and still have time to spare, focus on the less important things.

It's easy to feel overwhelmed if too many crucial tasks demand your attention on any given day. However, it's important to remember that you have supportive loved ones who can help you. Therefore, it may be possible to save time completing your tasks if you can ask for favours from them. Because of this, you'll have more time to focus on other important tasks.

You can only rely on your memory to keep some of the details of your daily agenda straight. So, you'll want to commit it to paper. It's a good idea to spend a few minutes at the end of each day creating a timetable for the following day. Also, while at it, see if you missed any opportunities that day. Then, schedule these things first thing tomorrow. This will provide you with a plan to follow to stay focused.

You should remember these items to enhance your capacity for time management. Take them to heart to effect lasting change in your life.

Conclusion

Effective time management is crucial for success in all aspects of life, including job and school. This is supported by the common knowledge that many highly effective people also possess exceptional time management skills. It may be challenging initially, but you will eventually learn to stick to schedules. You may evaluate how successfully you stuck to your plan by reviewing your program at the end of each day. The impact of time management on your life will become increasingly apparent as the number of chores you complete each day grows. You'll feel better about yourself and be able to perform better under stress if you do this.

You can now begin scheduling your time and life with the help of these guidelines and a good planner.

Dan Ford.
London, May 2023.

Daily Planner

DAY PLANNER

Date: ....

To do List

- ☐ ....
- ☐ ....
- ☐ ....
- ☐ ....
- ☐ ....
- ☐ ....
- ☐ ....
- ☐ ....
- ☐ ....
- ☐ ....
- ☐ ....
- ☐ ....
- ☐ ....
- ☐ ....
- ☐ ....

Priorities

Enthusiastic for

Appointments

- ☐ ....
- ☐ ....
- ☐ ....
- ☐ ....
- ☐ ....

Breakfast

Lunch

Dinner

Snacks

Fitness

- ☐ ....
- ☐ ....
- ☐ ....

Mood

☺ ☺ ☹

☐ ....

DAY PLANNER

Date: ....

To do List

- ☐ ....
- ☐ ....
- ☐ ....
- ☐ ....
- ☐ ....
- ☐ ....
- ☐ ....
- ☐ ....
- ☐ ....
- ☐ ....
- ☐ ....
- ☐ ....
- ☐ ....
- ☐ ....
- ☐ ....
- ☐ ....

Priorities

Enthusiastic for

Appointments

- ☐ ....
- ☐ ....
- ☐ ....
- ☐ ....
- ☐ ....

Breakfast

Lunch

Dinner

Snacks

Fitness

- ☐ ....
- ☐ ....
- ☐ ....

Mood

☺ ☺ ☹

☐ ....

DAY PLANNER

Date: ....

To do List

- ☐ ....
- ☐ ....
- ☐ ....
- ☐ ....
- ☐ ....
- ☐ ....
- ☐ ....
- ☐ ....
- ☐ ....
- ☐ ....
- ☐ ....
- ☐ ....
- ☐ ....
- ☐ ....
- ☐ ....
- ☐ ....

Priorities

Enthusiastic for

Appointments

- ☐ ....
- ☐ ....
- ☐ ....
- ☐ ....
- ☐ ....

Breakfast

Lunch

Dinner

Snacks

Fitness

- ☐ ....
- ☐ ....
- ☐ ....

Mood

☺ ☐ ☹

☐ ....

DAY PLANNER

Date: ....

To do List

- ☐ ....
- ☐ ....
- ☐ ....
- ☐ ....
- ☐ ....
- ☐ ....
- ☐ ....
- ☐ ....
- ☐ ....
- ☐ ....
- ☐ ....
- ☐ ....
- ☐ ....
- ☐ ....
- ☐ ....
- ☐ ....

Priorities

Enthusiastic for

Appointments

- ☐ ....
- ☐ ....
- ☐ ....
- ☐ ....
- ☐ ....

Breakfast   ## Lunch   ## Dinner   ## Snacks

Fitness

- ☐ ....
- ☐ ....
- ☐ ....

Mood

☺ ☺ ☹

☐ ....

DAY PLANNER

Date: ....

To do List

- ☐ ....
- ☐ ....
- ☐ ....
- ☐ ....
- ☐ ....
- ☐ ....
- ☐ ....
- ☐ ....
- ☐ ....
- ☐ ....
- ☐ ....
- ☐ ....
- ☐ ....
- ☐ ....
- ☐ ....
- ☐ ....

Priorities

Enthusiastic for

Appointments

- ☐ ....
- ☐ ....
- ☐ ....
- ☐ ....
- ☐ ....

Breakfast	Lunch	Dinner	Snacks

Fitness

- ☐ ....
- ☐ ....
- ☐ ....

Mood

☺   😐   ☹

☐ ....

DAY PLANNER

Date: ....

To do List

- ☐ ....
- ☐ ....
- ☐ ....
- ☐ ....
- ☐ ....
- ☐ ....
- ☐ ....
- ☐ ....
- ☐ ....
- ☐ ....
- ☐ ....
- ☐ ....
- ☐ ....
- ☐ ....
- ☐ ....
- ☐ ....

Priorities

Enthusiastic for

Appointments

- ☐ ....
- ☐ ....
- ☐ ....
- ☐ ....
- ☐ ....

Breakfast

Lunch

Dinner

Snacks

Fitness

- ☐ ....
- ☐ ....
- ☐ ....

Mood

☺ ☺ ☹

☐ ....

DAY PLANNER

Date: ....

To do List

- ☐ ....
- ☐ ....
- ☐ ....
- ☐ ....
- ☐ ....
- ☐ ....
- ☐ ....
- ☐ ....
- ☐ ....
- ☐ ....
- ☐ ....
- ☐ ....
- ☐ ....
- ☐ ....
- ☐ ....
- ☐ ....

Priorities

Enthusiastic for

Appointments

- ☐ ....
- ☐ ....
- ☐ ....
- ☐ ....
- ☐ ....

Breakfast

Lunch

Dinner

Snacks

Fitness

- ☐ ....
- ☐ ....
- ☐ ....

Mood

☺   😐   ☹

☐   ....

DAY PLANNER

Date: ....

To do List

- ☐ ....
- ☐ ....
- ☐ ....
- ☐ ....
- ☐ ....
- ☐ ....
- ☐ ....
- ☐ ....
- ☐ ....
- ☐ ....
- ☐ ....
- ☐ ....
- ☐ ....
- ☐ ....
- ☐ ....
- ☐ ....

Priorities

Enthusiastic for

Appointments

- ☐ ....
- ☐ ....
- ☐ ....
- ☐ ....
- ☐ ....

Breakfast	Lunch	Dinner	Snacks

Fitness

- ☐ ....
- ☐ ....
- ☐ ....

Mood

☺ ☺ ☹

☐ ....

DAY PLANNER

Date: ....

To do List

- ☐ ....
- ☐ ....
- ☐ ....
- ☐ ....
- ☐ ....
- ☐ ....
- ☐ ....
- ☐ ....
- ☐ ....
- ☐ ....
- ☐ ....
- ☐ ....
- ☐ ....
- ☐ ....
- ☐ ....

Priorities

Enthusiastic for

Appointments

- ☐ ....
- ☐ ....
- ☐ ....
- ☐ ....
- ☐ ....

Breakfast

Lunch

Dinner

Snacks

Fitness

- ☐ ....
- ☐ ....
- ☐ ....

Mood

☺   ☺   ☹

☐ ....

DAY PLANNER

Date: ....

To do List

- [ ] ....
- [ ] ....
- [ ] ....
- [ ] ....
- [ ] ....
- [ ] ....
- [ ] ....
- [ ] ....
- [ ] ....
- [ ] ....
- [ ] ....
- [ ] ....
- [ ] ....
- [ ] ....
- [ ] ....
- [ ] ....

Priorities

Enthusiastic for

Appointments

- [ ] ....
- [ ] ....
- [ ] ....
- [ ] ....
- [ ] ....

Breakfast

Lunch

Dinner

Snacks

Fitness

- [ ] ....
- [ ] ....
- [ ] ....

Mood

☺ ☻ ☹

- [ ] ....

DAY PLANNER

Date: ....

To do List

- [ ] ....
- [ ] ....
- [ ] ....
- [ ] ....
- [ ] ....
- [ ] ....
- [ ] ....
- [ ] ....
- [ ] ....
- [ ] ....
- [ ] ....
- [ ] ....
- [ ] ....
- [ ] ....
- [ ] ....
- [ ] ....

Priorities

Enthusiastic for

Appointments

- [ ] ....
- [ ] ....
- [ ] ....
- [ ] ....
- [ ] ....

Breakfast

Lunch

Dinner

Snacks

Fitness

- [ ] ....
- [ ] ....
- [ ] ....

Mood

☺   😐   ☹

- [ ] ....

DAY PLANNER

Date: ....

To do List

- ☐ ....
- ☐ ....
- ☐ ....
- ☐ ....
- ☐ ....
- ☐ ....
- ☐ ....
- ☐ ....
- ☐ ....
- ☐ ....
- ☐ ....
- ☐ ....
- ☐ ....
- ☐ ....
- ☐ ....
- ☐ ....

Priorities

Enthusiastic for

Appointments

- ☐ ....
- ☐ ....
- ☐ ....
- ☐ ....
- ☐ ....

Breakfast

Lunch

Dinner

Snacks

Fitness

- ☐ ....
- ☐ ....
- ☐ ....

Mood

☺   😐   ☹

☐ ....

DAY PLANNER

Date: ....

To do List

- ☐ ....
- ☐ ....
- ☐ ....
- ☐ ....
- ☐ ....
- ☐ ....
- ☐ ....
- ☐ ....
- ☐ ....
- ☐ ....
- ☐ ....
- ☐ ....
- ☐ ....
- ☐ ....
- ☐ ....
- ☐ ....

Priorities

Enthusiastic for

Appointments

- ☐ ....
- ☐ ....
- ☐ ....
- ☐ ....
- ☐ ....

Breakfast	Lunch	Dinner	Snacks

Fitness

- ☐ ....
- ☐ ....
- ☐ ....

Mood

☺ ☺ ☹

☐ ....

DAY PLANNER

Date: ....

To do List

- [ ] ....
- [ ] ....
- [ ] ....
- [ ] ....
- [ ] ....
- [ ] ....
- [ ] ....
- [ ] ....
- [ ] ....
- [ ] ....
- [ ] ....
- [ ] ....
- [ ] ....
- [ ] ....
- [ ] ....

Priorities

Enthusiastic for

Appointments

- [ ] ....
- [ ] ....
- [ ] ....
- [ ] ....
- [ ] ....

Breakfast

Lunch

Dinner

Snacks

Fitness

- [ ] ....
- [ ] ....
- [ ] ....

Mood

☺   ☻   ☹

- [ ] ....

DAY PLANNER

Date: ....

To do List

- [ ] ....
- [ ] ....
- [ ] ....
- [ ] ....
- [ ] ....
- [ ] ....
- [ ] ....
- [ ] ....
- [ ] ....
- [ ] ....
- [ ] ....
- [ ] ....
- [ ] ....
- [ ] ....
- [ ] ....
- [ ] ....

Priorities

Enthusiastic for

Appointments

- [ ] ....
- [ ] ....
- [ ] ....
- [ ] ....
- [ ] ....

Breakfast

Lunch

Dinner

Snacks

Fitness

- [ ] ....
- [ ] ....
- [ ] ....

Mood

☺ ☻ ☹

- [ ] ....

DAY PLANNER

Date: ....

To do List

- ☐ ....
- ☐ ....
- ☐ ....
- ☐ ....
- ☐ ....
- ☐ ....
- ☐ ....
- ☐ ....
- ☐ ....
- ☐ ....
- ☐ ....
- ☐ ....
- ☐ ....
- ☐ ....
- ☐ ....

Priorities

Enthusiastic for

Appointments

- ☐ ....
- ☐ ....
- ☐ ....
- ☐ ....
- ☐ ....

Breakfast

Lunch

Dinner

Snacks

Fitness

- ☐ ....
- ☐ ....
- ☐ ....

Mood

☺ ☺ ☹

☐ ....

DAY PLANNER

Date: ....

To do List

- [ ] ....
- [ ] ....
- [ ] ....
- [ ] ....
- [ ] ....
- [ ] ....
- [ ] ....
- [ ] ....
- [ ] ....
- [ ] ....
- [ ] ....
- [ ] ....
- [ ] ....
- [ ] ....
- [ ] ....
- [ ] ....

Priorities

Enthusiastic for

Appointments

- [ ] ....
- [ ] ....
- [ ] ....
- [ ] ....
- [ ] ....

Breakfast

Lunch

Dinner

Snacks

Fitness

- [ ] ....
- [ ] ....
- [ ] ....

Mood

☺ 😐 ☹

- [ ] ....

DAY PLANNER

Date: ....

To do List

- ☐ ....
- ☐ ....
- ☐ ....
- ☐ ....
- ☐ ....
- ☐ ....
- ☐ ....
- ☐ ....
- ☐ ....
- ☐ ....
- ☐ ....
- ☐ ....
- ☐ ....
- ☐ ....
- ☐ ....
- ☐ ....

Priorities

Enthusiastic for

Appointments

- ☐ ....
- ☐ ....
- ☐ ....
- ☐ ....
- ☐ ....

Breakfast

Lunch

Dinner

Snacks

Fitness

- ☐ ....
- ☐ ....
- ☐ ....

Mood

☺ ☻ ☹

☐ ....

DAY PLANNER

Date: ....

To do List

- ☐ ....
- ☐ ....
- ☐ ....
- ☐ ....
- ☐ ....
- ☐ ....
- ☐ ....
- ☐ ....
- ☐ ....
- ☐ ....
- ☐ ....
- ☐ ....
- ☐ ....
- ☐ ....
- ☐ ....

Priorities

Enthusiastic for

Appointments

- ☐ ....
- ☐ ....
- ☐ ....
- ☐ ....
- ☐ ....

Breakfast

Lunch

Dinner

Snacks

Fitness

- ☐ ....
- ☐ ....
- ☐ ....

Mood

☺ ☹ ☹

- ☐ ....

DAY PLANNER

Date: ....

To do List

- [ ] ....
- [ ] ....
- [ ] ....
- [ ] ....
- [ ] ....
- [ ] ....
- [ ] ....
- [ ] ....
- [ ] ....
- [ ] ....
- [ ] ....
- [ ] ....
- [ ] ....
- [ ] ....
- [ ] ....
- [ ] ....

Priorities

Enthusiastic for

Appointments

- [ ] ....
- [ ] ....
- [ ] ....
- [ ] ....
- [ ] ....

Breakfast

Lunch

Dinner

Snacks

Fitness

- [ ] ....
- [ ] ....
- [ ] ....

Mood

☺ 😐 ☹

- [ ] ....

DAY PLANNER

Date: ....

To do List

- ☐ ....
- ☐ ....
- ☐ ....
- ☐ ....
- ☐ ....
- ☐ ....
- ☐ ....
- ☐ ....
- ☐ ....
- ☐ ....
- ☐ ....
- ☐ ....
- ☐ ....
- ☐ ....
- ☐ ....
- ☐ ....

Priorities

Enthusiastic for

Appointments

- ☐ ....
- ☐ ....
- ☐ ....
- ☐ ....
- ☐ ....

Breakfast

Lunch

Dinner

Snacks

Fitness

- ☐ ....
- ☐ ....
- ☐ ....

Mood

☺ ☺ ☹

☐ ....

DAY PLANNER

Date: ....

To do List

- ☐ ....
- ☐ ....
- ☐ ....
- ☐ ....
- ☐ ....
- ☐ ....
- ☐ ....
- ☐ ....
- ☐ ....
- ☐ ....
- ☐ ....
- ☐ ....
- ☐ ....
- ☐ ....
- ☐ ....

Priorities

Enthusiastic for

Appointments

- ☐ ....
- ☐ ....
- ☐ ....
- ☐ ....
- ☐ ....

Breakfast

Lunch

Dinner

Snacks

Fitness

- ☐ ....
- ☐ ....
- ☐ ....

Mood

- ☐ ....

DAY PLANNER

Date: ....

To do List

- ☐ ....
- ☐ ....
- ☐ ....
- ☐ ....
- ☐ ....
- ☐ ....
- ☐ ....
- ☐ ....
- ☐ ....
- ☐ ....
- ☐ ....
- ☐ ....
- ☐ ....
- ☐ ....
- ☐ ....
- ☐ ....

Priorities

Enthusiastic for

Appointments

- ☐ ....
- ☐ ....
- ☐ ....
- ☐ ....
- ☐ ....

Breakfast

Lunch

Dinner

Snacks

Fitness

- ☐ ....
- ☐ ....
- ☐ ....

Mood

☺ ☐ ☹

☐ ....

DAY PLANNER

Date: ....

To do List

- ☐ ....
- ☐ ....
- ☐ ....
- ☐ ....
- ☐ ....
- ☐ ....
- ☐ ....
- ☐ ....
- ☐ ....
- ☐ ....
- ☐ ....
- ☐ ....
- ☐ ....
- ☐ ....
- ☐ ....
- ☐ ....

Priorities

Enthusiastic for

Appointments

- ☐ ....
- ☐ ....
- ☐ ....
- ☐ ....
- ☐ ....

Breakfast

Lunch

Dinner

Snacks

Fitness

- ☐ ....
- ☐ ....
- ☐ ....

Mood

☺ ☺ ☹

☐ ....

DAY PLANNER

Date: ....

To do List

- ☐ ....
- ☐ ....
- ☐ ....
- ☐ ....
- ☐ ....
- ☐ ....
- ☐ ....
- ☐ ....
- ☐ ....
- ☐ ....
- ☐ ....
- ☐ ....
- ☐ ....
- ☐ ....
- ☐ ....
- ☐ ....

Priorities

Enthusiastic for

Appointments

- ☐ ....
- ☐ ....
- ☐ ....
- ☐ ....
- ☐ ....

Breakfast | Lunch | Dinner | Snacks

Fitness

- ☐ ....
- ☐ ....
- ☐ ....

Mood

☺   😐   ☹

- ☐ ....

DAY PLANNER

Date: ....

To do List

- ☐ ....
- ☐ ....
- ☐ ....
- ☐ ....
- ☐ ....
- ☐ ....
- ☐ ....
- ☐ ....
- ☐ ....
- ☐ ....
- ☐ ....
- ☐ ....
- ☐ ....
- ☐ ....
- ☐ ....
- ☐ ....

Priorities

Enthusiastic for

Appointments

- ☐ ....
- ☐ ....
- ☐ ....
- ☐ ....
- ☐ ....

Breakfast

Lunch

Dinner

Snacks

Fitness

- ☐ ....
- ☐ ....
- ☐ ....

Mood

☺ ☺ ☹

☐ ....

DAY PLANNER

Date: ....

To do List

- ☐ ....
- ☐ ....
- ☐ ....
- ☐ ....
- ☐ ....
- ☐ ....
- ☐ ....
- ☐ ....
- ☐ ....
- ☐ ....
- ☐ ....
- ☐ ....
- ☐ ....
- ☐ ....
- ☐ ....

Priorities

Enthusiastic for

Appointments

- ☐ ....
- ☐ ....
- ☐ ....
- ☐ ....
- ☐ ....

Breakfast

Lunch

Dinner

Snacks

Fitness

- ☐ ....
- ☐ ....
- ☐ ....

Mood

☺   ☐   ☹

☐ ....

DAY PLANNER

Date: ....

To do List

- ☐ ....
- ☐ ....
- ☐ ....
- ☐ ....
- ☐ ....
- ☐ ....
- ☐ ....
- ☐ ....
- ☐ ....
- ☐ ....
- ☐ ....
- ☐ ....
- ☐ ....
- ☐ ....
- ☐ ....

Priorities

Enthusiastic for

Appointments

- ☐ ....
- ☐ ....
- ☐ ....
- ☐ ....
- ☐ ....

Breakfast

Lunch

Dinner

Snacks

Fitness

- ☐ ....
- ☐ ....
- ☐ ....

Mood

☺ ☺ ☹

☐ ....

DAY PLANNER

Date: ....

To do List

- [ ] ....
- [ ] ....
- [ ] ....
- [ ] ....
- [ ] ....
- [ ] ....
- [ ] ....
- [ ] ....
- [ ] ....
- [ ] ....
- [ ] ....
- [ ] ....
- [ ] ....
- [ ] ....
- [ ] ....
- [ ] ....

Priorities

Enthusiastic for

Appointments

- [ ] ....
- [ ] ....
- [ ] ....
- [ ] ....
- [ ] ....

Breakfast

Lunch

Dinner

Snacks

Fitness

- [ ] ....
- [ ] ....
- [ ] ....

Mood

😊 😐 ☹️

- [ ] ....

DAY PLANNER

Date: ....

To do List

- [ ] ....
- [ ] ....
- [ ] ....
- [ ] ....
- [ ] ....
- [ ] ....
- [ ] ....
- [ ] ....
- [ ] ....
- [ ] ....
- [ ] ....
- [ ] ....
- [ ] ....
- [ ] ....
- [ ] ....
- [ ] ....
- [ ] ....

Priorities

Enthusiastic for

Appointments

- [ ] ....
- [ ] ....
- [ ] ....
- [ ] ....
- [ ] ....

Breakfast

Lunch

Dinner

Snacks

Fitness

- [ ] ....
- [ ] ....
- [ ] ....

Mood

☺ ☺ ☹

- [ ] ....

DAY PLANNER

Date: ....

To do List

- ☐ ....
- ☐ ....
- ☐ ....
- ☐ ....
- ☐ ....
- ☐ ....
- ☐ ....
- ☐ ....
- ☐ ....
- ☐ ....
- ☐ ....
- ☐ ....
- ☐ ....
- ☐ ....
- ☐ ....
- ☐ ....

Priorities

Enthusiastic for

Appointments

- ☐ ....
- ☐ ....
- ☐ ....
- ☐ ....
- ☐ ....

Breakfast

Lunch

Dinner

Snacks

Fitness

- ☐ ....
- ☐ ....
- ☐ ....

Mood

☺   😐   ☹

☐ ....

DAY PLANNER

Date: ....

To do List

- ☐ ....
- ☐ ....
- ☐ ....
- ☐ ....
- ☐ ....
- ☐ ....
- ☐ ....
- ☐ ....
- ☐ ....
- ☐ ....
- ☐ ....
- ☐ ....
- ☐ ....
- ☐ ....
- ☐ ....
- ☐ ....

Priorities

Enthusiastic for

Appointments

- ☐ ....
- ☐ ....
- ☐ ....
- ☐ ....
- ☐ ....

Breakfast	Lunch	Dinner	Snacks

Fitness

- ☐ ....
- ☐ ....
- ☐ ....

Mood

☺   ☺   ☹

☐ ....

DAY PLANNER

Date: ....

To do List

- [ ] ....
- [ ] ....
- [ ] ....
- [ ] ....
- [ ] ....
- [ ] ....
- [ ] ....
- [ ] ....
- [ ] ....
- [ ] ....
- [ ] ....
- [ ] ....
- [ ] ....
- [ ] ....
- [ ] ....

Priorities

Enthusiastic for

Appointments

- [ ] ....
- [ ] ....
- [ ] ....
- [ ] ....
- [ ] ....

Breakfast

Lunch

Dinner

Snacks

Fitness

- [ ] ....
- [ ] ....
- [ ] ....

Mood

☺   😐   ☹

- [ ] ....

DAY PLANNER

Date: ....

To do List

- ☐ ....
- ☐ ....
- ☐ ....
- ☐ ....
- ☐ ....
- ☐ ....
- ☐ ....
- ☐ ....
- ☐ ....
- ☐ ....
- ☐ ....
- ☐ ....
- ☐ ....
- ☐ ....
- ☐ ....
- ☐ ....

Priorities

Enthusiastic for

Appointments

- ☐ ....
- ☐ ....
- ☐ ....
- ☐ ....
- ☐ ....

Breakfast   Lunch   Dinner   Snacks

Fitness

- ☐ ....
- ☐ ....
- ☐ ....

Mood

☺ ☺ ☹

☐ ....

DAY PLANNER

Date: ....

To do List

- ☐ ....
- ☐ ....
- ☐ ....
- ☐ ....
- ☐ ....
- ☐ ....
- ☐ ....
- ☐ ....
- ☐ ....
- ☐ ....
- ☐ ....
- ☐ ....
- ☐ ....
- ☐ ....
- ☐ ....

Priorities

Enthusiastic for

Appointments

- ☐ ....
- ☐ ....
- ☐ ....
- ☐ ....
- ☐ ....

Breakfast

Lunch

Dinner

Snacks

Fitness

- ☐ ....
- ☐ ....
- ☐ ....

Mood

☺   ☹   ☹

☐ ....

DAY PLANNER

Date: ....

To do List

- ☐ ....
- ☐ ....
- ☐ ....
- ☐ ....
- ☐ ....
- ☐ ....
- ☐ ....
- ☐ ....
- ☐ ....
- ☐ ....
- ☐ ....
- ☐ ....
- ☐ ....
- ☐ ....
- ☐ ....
- ☐ ....

Priorities

Enthusiastic for

Appointments

- ☐ ....
- ☐ ....
- ☐ ....
- ☐ ....
- ☐ ....

Breakfast

Lunch

Dinner

Snacks

Fitness

- ☐ ....
- ☐ ....
- ☐ ....

Mood

☺ 😐 ☹

☐ ....

DAY PLANNER

Date: ....

To do List

- ☐ ....
- ☐ ....
- ☐ ....
- ☐ ....
- ☐ ....
- ☐ ....
- ☐ ....
- ☐ ....
- ☐ ....
- ☐ ....
- ☐ ....
- ☐ ....
- ☐ ....
- ☐ ....
- ☐ ....
- ☐ ....

Priorities

Enthusiastic for

Appointments

- ☐ ....
- ☐ ....
- ☐ ....
- ☐ ....
- ☐ ....

Breakfast

Lunch

Dinner

Snacks

Fitness

- ☐ ....
- ☐ ....
- ☐ ....

Mood

☺ ☺ ☹

☐ ....

DAY PLANNER

Date: ....

To do List

- ☐ ....
- ☐ ....
- ☐ ....
- ☐ ....
- ☐ ....
- ☐ ....
- ☐ ....
- ☐ ....
- ☐ ....
- ☐ ....
- ☐ ....
- ☐ ....
- ☐ ....
- ☐ ....
- ☐ ....
- ☐ ....

Priorities

Enthusiastic for

Appointments

- ☐ ....
- ☐ ....
- ☐ ....
- ☐ ....
- ☐ ....

Breakfast

Lunch

Dinner

Snacks

Fitness

- ☐ ....
- ☐ ....
- ☐ ....

Mood

☺   😐   ☹

☐ ....

DAY PLANNER

Date: ....

To do List

- ☐ ....
- ☐ ....
- ☐ ....
- ☐ ....
- ☐ ....
- ☐ ....
- ☐ ....
- ☐ ....
- ☐ ....
- ☐ ....
- ☐ ....
- ☐ ....
- ☐ ....
- ☐ ....
- ☐ ....

Priorities

Enthusiastic for

Appointments

- ☐ ....
- ☐ ....
- ☐ ....
- ☐ ....
- ☐ ....

Breakfast   ## Lunch   ## Dinner   ## Snacks

Fitness

- ☐ ....
- ☐ ....
- ☐ ....

Mood

☺   ☺   ☹

☐ ....

DAY PLANNER

Date: ....

To do List

- ☐ ....
- ☐ ....
- ☐ ....
- ☐ ....
- ☐ ....
- ☐ ....
- ☐ ....
- ☐ ....
- ☐ ....
- ☐ ....
- ☐ ....
- ☐ ....
- ☐ ....
- ☐ ....
- ☐ ....
- ☐ ....

Priorities

Enthusiastic for

Appointments

- ☐ ....
- ☐ ....
- ☐ ....
- ☐ ....
- ☐ ....

Breakfast

Lunch

Dinner

Snacks

Fitness

- ☐ ....
- ☐ ....
- ☐ ....

Mood

☺ 😐 ☹

☐ ....

DAY PLANNER

Date: ....

To do List

- ☐ ....
- ☐ ....
- ☐ ....
- ☐ ....
- ☐ ....
- ☐ ....
- ☐ ....
- ☐ ....
- ☐ ....
- ☐ ....
- ☐ ....
- ☐ ....
- ☐ ....
- ☐ ....
- ☐ ....

Priorities

Enthusiastic for

Appointments

- ☐ ....
- ☐ ....
- ☐ ....
- ☐ ....
- ☐ ....

Breakfast

Lunch

Dinner

Snacks

Fitness

- ☐ ....
- ☐ ....
- ☐ ....

Mood

☺   ☺   ☹

☐ ....

DAY PLANNER

Date: ....

To do List

- [ ] ....
- [ ] ....
- [ ] ....
- [ ] ....
- [ ] ....
- [ ] ....
- [ ] ....
- [ ] ....
- [ ] ....
- [ ] ....
- [ ] ....
- [ ] ....
- [ ] ....
- [ ] ....
- [ ] ....
- [ ] ....

Priorities

Enthusiastic for

Appointments

- [ ] ....
- [ ] ....
- [ ] ....
- [ ] ....
- [ ] ....

Breakfast

Lunch

Dinner

Snacks

Fitness

- [ ] ....
- [ ] ....
- [ ] ....

Mood

☺ ☺ ☹

- [ ] ....

DAY PLANNER

Date: ....

To do List

- [ ] ....
- [ ] ....
- [ ] ....
- [ ] ....
- [ ] ....
- [ ] ....
- [ ] ....
- [ ] ....
- [ ] ....
- [ ] ....
- [ ] ....
- [ ] ....
- [ ] ....
- [ ] ....
- [ ] ....
- [ ] ....

Priorities

Enthusiastic for

Appointments

- [ ] ....
- [ ] ....
- [ ] ....
- [ ] ....
- [ ] ....

Breakfast

Lunch

Dinner

Snacks

Fitness

- [ ] ....
- [ ] ....
- [ ] ....

Mood

☺ ☺ ☹

- [ ] ....

DAY PLANNER

Date: ....

To do List

- ☐ ....
- ☐ ....
- ☐ ....
- ☐ ....
- ☐ ....
- ☐ ....
- ☐ ....
- ☐ ....
- ☐ ....
- ☐ ....
- ☐ ....
- ☐ ....
- ☐ ....
- ☐ ....
- ☐ ....

Priorities

Enthusiastic for

Appointments

- ☐ ....
- ☐ ....
- ☐ ....
- ☐ ....
- ☐ ....

Breakfast

Lunch

Dinner

Snacks

Fitness

- ☐ ....
- ☐ ....
- ☐ ....

Mood

☺ ☐ ☹

- ☐ ....

DAY PLANNER

Date: ....

To do List

- ☐ ....
- ☐ ....
- ☐ ....
- ☐ ....
- ☐ ....
- ☐ ....
- ☐ ....
- ☐ ....
- ☐ ....
- ☐ ....
- ☐ ....
- ☐ ....
- ☐ ....
- ☐ ....
- ☐ ....
- ☐ ....

Priorities

Enthusiastic for

Appointments

- ☐ ....
- ☐ ....
- ☐ ....
- ☐ ....
- ☐ ....

Breakfast

Lunch

Dinner

Snacks

Fitness

- ☐ ....
- ☐ ....
- ☐ ....

Mood

☺ ☺ ☹

☐ ....

DAY PLANNER

Date: ....

To do List

- ☐ ....
- ☐ ....
- ☐ ....
- ☐ ....
- ☐ ....
- ☐ ....
- ☐ ....
- ☐ ....
- ☐ ....
- ☐ ....
- ☐ ....
- ☐ ....
- ☐ ....
- ☐ ....
- ☐ ....

Priorities

Enthusiastic for

Appointments

- ☐ ....
- ☐ ....
- ☐ ....
- ☐ ....
- ☐ ....

Breakfast

Lunch

Dinner

Snacks

Fitness

- ☐ ....
- ☐ ....
- ☐ ....

Mood

☺ ☺ ☹

☐ ....

DAY PLANNER

Date: ....

To do List

- ☐ ....
- ☐ ....
- ☐ ....
- ☐ ....
- ☐ ....
- ☐ ....
- ☐ ....
- ☐ ....
- ☐ ....
- ☐ ....
- ☐ ....
- ☐ ....
- ☐ ....
- ☐ ....
- ☐ ....
- ☐ ....

Priorities

Enthusiastic for

Appointments

- ☐ ....
- ☐ ....
- ☐ ....
- ☐ ....
- ☐ ....

Breakfast

Lunch

Dinner

Snacks

Fitness

- ☐ ....
- ☐ ....
- ☐ ....

Mood

☺ ☺ ☹

☐ ....

DAY PLANNER

Date: ....

To do List

- ☐ ....
- ☐ ....
- ☐ ....
- ☐ ....
- ☐ ....
- ☐ ....
- ☐ ....
- ☐ ....
- ☐ ....
- ☐ ....
- ☐ ....
- ☐ ....
- ☐ ....
- ☐ ....
- ☐ ....
- ☐ ....

Priorities

Enthusiastic for

Appointments

- ☐ ....
- ☐ ....
- ☐ ....
- ☐ ....
- ☐ ....

Breakfast

Lunch

Dinner

Snacks

Fitness

- ☐ ....
- ☐ ....
- ☐ ....

Mood

☺   😐   ☹

☐ ....

DAY PLANNER

Date: ....

To do List

- ☐ ....
- ☐ ....
- ☐ ....
- ☐ ....
- ☐ ....
- ☐ ....
- ☐ ....
- ☐ ....
- ☐ ....
- ☐ ....
- ☐ ....
- ☐ ....
- ☐ ....
- ☐ ....
- ☐ ....

Priorities

Enthusiastic for

Appointments

- ☐ ....
- ☐ ....
- ☐ ....
- ☐ ....
- ☐ ....

Breakfast

Lunch

Dinner

Snacks

Fitness

- ☐ ....
- ☐ ....
- ☐ ....

Mood

☺   😐   ☹

☐ ....

DAY PLANNER

Date: ....

To do List

- ☐ ....
- ☐ ....
- ☐ ....
- ☐ ....
- ☐ ....
- ☐ ....
- ☐ ....
- ☐ ....
- ☐ ....
- ☐ ....
- ☐ ....
- ☐ ....
- ☐ ....
- ☐ ....
- ☐ ....
- ☐ ....

Priorities

Enthusiastic for

Appointments

- ☐ ....
- ☐ ....
- ☐ ....
- ☐ ....
- ☐ ....

Breakfast

Lunch

Dinner

Snacks

Fitness

- ☐ ....
- ☐ ....
- ☐ ....

Mood

☐ ....

DAY PLANNER

Date: ....

To do List

- ☐ ....
- ☐ ....
- ☐ ....
- ☐ ....
- ☐ ....
- ☐ ....
- ☐ ....
- ☐ ....
- ☐ ....
- ☐ ....
- ☐ ....
- ☐ ....
- ☐ ....
- ☐ ....
- ☐ ....

Priorities

Enthusiastic for

Appointments

- ☐ ....
- ☐ ....
- ☐ ....
- ☐ ....
- ☐ ....

Breakfast

Lunch

Dinner

Snacks

Fitness

- ☐ ....
- ☐ ....
- ☐ ....

Mood

☺   ☐   ☹

☐ ....

DAY PLANNER

Date: ....

To do List

☐ ....
☐ ....
☐ ....
☐ ....
☐ ....
☐ ....
☐ ....
☐ ....
☐ ....
☐ ....
☐ ....
☐ ....
☐ ....
☐ ....
☐ ....

Priorities

Enthusiastic for

Appointments

☐ ....
☐ ....
☐ ....
☐ ....
☐ ....

Breakfast

Lunch

Dinner

Snacks

Fitness

☐ ....
☐ ....
☐ ....

Mood

☺ 😐 ☹

☐ ....

DAY PLANNER

Date: ....

To do List

- ☐ ....
- ☐ ....
- ☐ ....
- ☐ ....
- ☐ ....
- ☐ ....
- ☐ ....
- ☐ ....
- ☐ ....
- ☐ ....
- ☐ ....
- ☐ ....
- ☐ ....
- ☐ ....
- ☐ ....
- ☐ ....

Priorities

Enthusiastic for

Appointments

- ☐ ....
- ☐ ....
- ☐ ....
- ☐ ....
- ☐ ....

Breakfast

Lunch

Dinner

Snacks

Fitness

- ☐ ....
- ☐ ....
- ☐ ....

Mood

☺   ☺   ☹

☐ ....

DAY PLANNER

Date: ....

To do List

- [ ] ....
- [ ] ....
- [ ] ....
- [ ] ....
- [ ] ....
- [ ] ....
- [ ] ....
- [ ] ....
- [ ] ....
- [ ] ....
- [ ] ....
- [ ] ....
- [ ] ....
- [ ] ....
- [ ] ....
- [ ] ....

Priorities

Enthusiastic for

Appointments

- [ ] ....
- [ ] ....
- [ ] ....
- [ ] ....
- [ ] ....

Breakfast

Lunch

Dinner

Snacks

Fitness

- [ ] ....
- [ ] ....
- [ ] ....

Mood

☺   😐   ☹

- [ ] ....

DAY PLANNER

Date: ....

To do List

- [ ] ....
- [ ] ....
- [ ] ....
- [ ] ....
- [ ] ....
- [ ] ....
- [ ] ....
- [ ] ....
- [ ] ....
- [ ] ....
- [ ] ....
- [ ] ....
- [ ] ....
- [ ] ....
- [ ] ....
- [ ] ....

Priorities

Enthusiastic for

Appointments

- [ ] ....
- [ ] ....
- [ ] ....
- [ ] ....
- [ ] ....

Breakfast

Lunch

Dinner

Snacks

Fitness

- [ ] ....
- [ ] ....
- [ ] ....

Mood

☺ ☺ ☹

- [ ] ....

DAY PLANNER

Date: ....

To do List

- ☐ ....
- ☐ ....
- ☐ ....
- ☐ ....
- ☐ ....
- ☐ ....
- ☐ ....
- ☐ ....
- ☐ ....
- ☐ ....
- ☐ ....
- ☐ ....
- ☐ ....
- ☐ ....
- ☐ ....
- ☐ ....

Priorities

Enthusiastic for

Appointments

- ☐ ....
- ☐ ....
- ☐ ....
- ☐ ....
- ☐ ....

Breakfast

Lunch

Dinner

Snacks

Fitness

- ☐ ....
- ☐ ....
- ☐ ....

Mood

☺ 😐 ☹

☐ ....

DAY PLANNER

Date: ....

To do List

- ☐ ....
- ☐ ....
- ☐ ....
- ☐ ....
- ☐ ....
- ☐ ....
- ☐ ....
- ☐ ....
- ☐ ....
- ☐ ....
- ☐ ....
- ☐ ....
- ☐ ....
- ☐ ....
- ☐ ....

Priorities

Enthusiastic for

Appointments

- ☐ ....
- ☐ ....
- ☐ ....
- ☐ ....
- ☐ ....

Breakfast

Lunch

Dinner

Snacks

Fitness

- ☐ ....
- ☐ ....
- ☐ ....

Mood

☺ ☺ ☹

- ☐ ....

DAY PLANNER

Date: ....

To do List

- [ ] ....
- [ ] ....
- [ ] ....
- [ ] ....
- [ ] ....
- [ ] ....
- [ ] ....
- [ ] ....
- [ ] ....
- [ ] ....
- [ ] ....
- [ ] ....
- [ ] ....
- [ ] ....
- [ ] ....
- [ ] ....

Priorities

Enthusiastic for

Appointments

- [ ] ....
- [ ] ....
- [ ] ....
- [ ] ....
- [ ] ....

Breakfast

Lunch

Dinner

Snacks

Fitness

- [ ] ....
- [ ] ....
- [ ] ....

Mood

☺ ☺ ☹

- [ ] ....

DAY PLANNER

Date: ....

To do List

☐ ....
☐ ....
☐ ....
☐ ....
☐ ....
☐ ....
☐ ....
☐ ....
☐ ....
☐ ....
☐ ....
☐ ....
☐ ....
☐ ....
☐ ....
☐ ....

Priorities

Enthusiastic for

Appointments

☐ ....
☐ ....
☐ ....
☐ ....
☐ ....

Breakfast

Lunch

Dinner

Snacks

Fitness

☐ ....
☐ ....
☐ ....

Mood

☺ ☺ ☹

☐ ....

DAY PLANNER

Date: ....

To do List

- ☐ ....
- ☐ ....
- ☐ ....
- ☐ ....
- ☐ ....
- ☐ ....
- ☐ ....
- ☐ ....
- ☐ ....
- ☐ ....
- ☐ ....
- ☐ ....
- ☐ ....
- ☐ ....
- ☐ ....
- ☐ ....

Priorities

Enthusiastic for

Appointments

- ☐ ....
- ☐ ....
- ☐ ....
- ☐ ....
- ☐ ....

Breakfast

Lunch

Dinner

Snacks

Fitness

- ☐ ....
- ☐ ....
- ☐ ....

Mood

☺ ☺ ☹

☐ ....

DAY PLANNER

Date: ....

To do List

- [ ] ....
- [ ] ....
- [ ] ....
- [ ] ....
- [ ] ....
- [ ] ....
- [ ] ....
- [ ] ....
- [ ] ....
- [ ] ....
- [ ] ....
- [ ] ....
- [ ] ....
- [ ] ....
- [ ] ....

Priorities

Enthusiastic for

Appointments

- [ ] ....
- [ ] ....
- [ ] ....
- [ ] ....
- [ ] ....

Breakfast

Lunch

Dinner

Snacks

Fitness

- [ ] ....
- [ ] ....
- [ ] ....

Mood

☺ ☺ ☹

- [ ] ....

DAY PLANNER

Date: ....

To do List

- [ ] ....
- [ ] ....
- [ ] ....
- [ ] ....
- [ ] ....
- [ ] ....
- [ ] ....
- [ ] ....
- [ ] ....
- [ ] ....
- [ ] ....
- [ ] ....
- [ ] ....
- [ ] ....
- [ ] ....
- [ ] ....

Priorities

Enthusiastic for

Appointments

- [ ] ....
- [ ] ....
- [ ] ....
- [ ] ....
- [ ] ....

Breakfast

Lunch

Dinner

Snacks

Fitness

- [ ] ....
- [ ] ....
- [ ] ....

Mood

☺ ☺ ☹

- [ ] ....

DAY PLANNER

Date: ....

To do List

- ☐ ....
- ☐ ....
- ☐ ....
- ☐ ....
- ☐ ....
- ☐ ....
- ☐ ....
- ☐ ....
- ☐ ....
- ☐ ....
- ☐ ....
- ☐ ....
- ☐ ....
- ☐ ....
- ☐ ....
- ☐ ....

Priorities

Enthusiastic for

Appointments

- ☐ ....
- ☐ ....
- ☐ ....
- ☐ ....
- ☐ ....

Breakfast

Lunch

Dinner

Snacks

Fitness

- ☐ ....
- ☐ ....
- ☐ ....

Mood

☺   ☐   ☹

☐ ....

DAY PLANNER

Date: ....

To do List

- ☐ ....
- ☐ ....
- ☐ ....
- ☐ ....
- ☐ ....
- ☐ ....
- ☐ ....
- ☐ ....
- ☐ ....
- ☐ ....
- ☐ ....
- ☐ ....
- ☐ ....
- ☐ ....
- ☐ ....
- ☐ ....
- ☐ ....

Priorities

Enthusiastic for

Appointments

- ☐ ....
- ☐ ....
- ☐ ....
- ☐ ....
- ☐ ....

Breakfast

Lunch

Dinner

Snacks

Fitness

- ☐ ....
- ☐ ....
- ☐ ....

Mood

☺   ☺   ☹

☐ ....

DAY PLANNER

Date: ....

To do List

- ☐ ....
- ☐ ....
- ☐ ....
- ☐ ....
- ☐ ....
- ☐ ....
- ☐ ....
- ☐ ....
- ☐ ....
- ☐ ....
- ☐ ....
- ☐ ....
- ☐ ....
- ☐ ....
- ☐ ....
- ☐ ....

Priorities

Enthusiastic for

Appointments

- ☐ ....
- ☐ ....
- ☐ ....
- ☐ ....
- ☐ ....

Breakfast	Lunch	Dinner	Snacks

Fitness

- ☐ ....
- ☐ ....
- ☐ ....

Mood

☺ ☻ ☹

☐ ....

DAY PLANNER

Date: ....

To do List

- ☐ ....
- ☐ ....
- ☐ ....
- ☐ ....
- ☐ ....
- ☐ ....
- ☐ ....
- ☐ ....
- ☐ ....
- ☐ ....
- ☐ ....
- ☐ ....
- ☐ ....
- ☐ ....
- ☐ ....
- ☐ ....

Priorities

Enthusiastic for

Appointments

- ☐ ....
- ☐ ....
- ☐ ....
- ☐ ....
- ☐ ....

Breakfast

Lunch

Dinner

Snacks

Fitness

- ☐ ....
- ☐ ....
- ☐ ....

Mood

☺ ☻ ☹

☐ ....

DAY PLANNER

Date: ....

To do List

- ☐ ....
- ☐ ....
- ☐ ....
- ☐ ....
- ☐ ....
- ☐ ....
- ☐ ....
- ☐ ....
- ☐ ....
- ☐ ....
- ☐ ....
- ☐ ....
- ☐ ....
- ☐ ....
- ☐ ....
- ☐ ....

Priorities

Enthusiastic for

Appointments

- ☐ ....
- ☐ ....
- ☐ ....
- ☐ ....
- ☐ ....

Breakfast

Lunch

Dinner

Snacks

Fitness

- ☐ ....
- ☐ ....
- ☐ ....

Mood

☺ ☺ ☹

☐ ....

DAY PLANNER

Date: ....

To do List

- ☐ ....
- ☐ ....
- ☐ ....
- ☐ ....
- ☐ ....
- ☐ ....
- ☐ ....
- ☐ ....
- ☐ ....
- ☐ ....
- ☐ ....
- ☐ ....
- ☐ ....
- ☐ ....
- ☐ ....
- ☐ ....

Priorities

Enthusiastic for

Appointments

- ☐ ....
- ☐ ....
- ☐ ....
- ☐ ....
- ☐ ....

Breakfast

Lunch

Dinner

Snacks

Fitness

- ☐ ....
- ☐ ....
- ☐ ....

Mood

☺ ☻ ☹

☐ ....

DAY PLANNER

Date: ....

To do List

- ☐ ....
- ☐ ....
- ☐ ....
- ☐ ....
- ☐ ....
- ☐ ....
- ☐ ....
- ☐ ....
- ☐ ....
- ☐ ....
- ☐ ....
- ☐ ....
- ☐ ....
- ☐ ....
- ☐ ....
- ☐ ....

Priorities

Enthusiastic for

Appointments

- ☐ ....
- ☐ ....
- ☐ ....
- ☐ ....
- ☐ ....

Breakfast

Lunch

Dinner

Snacks

Fitness

- ☐ ....
- ☐ ....
- ☐ ....

Mood

☺   ☻   ☹

- ☐ ....

DAY PLANNER

Date: ....

To do List

- ☐ ....
- ☐ ....
- ☐ ....
- ☐ ....
- ☐ ....
- ☐ ....
- ☐ ....
- ☐ ....
- ☐ ....
- ☐ ....
- ☐ ....
- ☐ ....
- ☐ ....
- ☐ ....
- ☐ ....
- ☐ ....

Priorities

Enthusiastic for

Appointments

- ☐ ....
- ☐ ....
- ☐ ....
- ☐ ....
- ☐ ....

Breakfast	Lunch	Dinner	Snacks

Fitness

- ☐ ....
- ☐ ....
- ☐ ....

Mood

☺   ☻   ☹

☐ ....

DAY PLANNER

Date: ....

To do List

- ☐ ....
- ☐ ....
- ☐ ....
- ☐ ....
- ☐ ....
- ☐ ....
- ☐ ....
- ☐ ....
- ☐ ....
- ☐ ....
- ☐ ....
- ☐ ....
- ☐ ....
- ☐ ....
- ☐ ....
- ☐ ....

Priorities

Enthusiastic for

Appointments

- ☐ ....
- ☐ ....
- ☐ ....
- ☐ ....
- ☐ ....

Breakfast

Lunch

Dinner

Snacks

Fitness

- ☐ ....
- ☐ ....
- ☐ ....

Mood

☺ ☹ ☹

- ☐ ....

DAY PLANNER

Date: ....

To do List

- ☐ ....
- ☐ ....
- ☐ ....
- ☐ ....
- ☐ ....
- ☐ ....
- ☐ ....
- ☐ ....
- ☐ ....
- ☐ ....
- ☐ ....
- ☐ ....
- ☐ ....
- ☐ ....
- ☐ ....
- ☐ ....

Priorities

Enthusiastic for

Appointments

- ☐ ....
- ☐ ....
- ☐ ....
- ☐ ....
- ☐ ....

Breakfast

Lunch

Dinner

Snacks

Fitness

- ☐ ....
- ☐ ....
- ☐ ....

Mood

☺ ☻ ☹

☐ ....

DAY PLANNER

Date: ....

To do List

- ☐ ....
- ☐ ....
- ☐ ....
- ☐ ....
- ☐ ....
- ☐ ....
- ☐ ....
- ☐ ....
- ☐ ....
- ☐ ....
- ☐ ....
- ☐ ....
- ☐ ....
- ☐ ....
- ☐ ....

Priorities

Enthusiastic for

Appointments

- ☐ ....
- ☐ ....
- ☐ ....
- ☐ ....
- ☐ ....

Breakfast

Lunch

Dinner

Snacks

Fitness

- ☐ ....
- ☐ ....
- ☐ ....

Mood

☺ 😐 ☹

- ☐ ....

DAY PLANNER

Date: ....

To do List

- ☐ ....
- ☐ ....
- ☐ ....
- ☐ ....
- ☐ ....
- ☐ ....
- ☐ ....
- ☐ ....
- ☐ ....
- ☐ ....
- ☐ ....
- ☐ ....
- ☐ ....
- ☐ ....
- ☐ ....

Priorities

Enthusiastic for

Appointments

- ☐ ....
- ☐ ....
- ☐ ....
- ☐ ....
- ☐ ....

Breakfast

Lunch

Dinner

Snacks

Fitness

- ☐ ....
- ☐ ....
- ☐ ....

Mood

☺   ☺   ☹

☐ ....

DAY PLANNER

Date: ....

To do List

☐ ....
☐ ....
☐ ....
☐ ....
☐ ....
☐ ....
☐ ....
☐ ....
☐ ....
☐ ....
☐ ....
☐ ....
☐ ....
☐ ....
☐ ....
☐ ....

Priorities

Enthusiastic for

Appointments

☐ ....
☐ ....
☐ ....
☐ ....
☐ ....

Breakfast

Lunch

Dinner

Snacks

Fitness

☐ ....
☐ ....
☐ ....

Mood

☺   😐   ☹

☐ ....

DAY PLANNER

Date: ....

To do List

- ☐ ....
- ☐ ....
- ☐ ....
- ☐ ....
- ☐ ....
- ☐ ....
- ☐ ....
- ☐ ....
- ☐ ....
- ☐ ....
- ☐ ....
- ☐ ....
- ☐ ....
- ☐ ....
- ☐ ....
- ☐ ....

Priorities

Enthusiastic for

Appointments

- ☐ ....
- ☐ ....
- ☐ ....
- ☐ ....
- ☐

Breakfast

Lunch

Dinner

Snacks

Fitness

- ☐ ....
- ☐ ....
- ☐ ....

Mood

☺   ☺   ☹

☐ ....

DAY PLANNER

Date: ....

To do List

- ☐ ....
- ☐ ....
- ☐ ....
- ☐ ....
- ☐ ....
- ☐ ....
- ☐ ....
- ☐ ....
- ☐ ....
- ☐ ....
- ☐ ....
- ☐ ....
- ☐ ....
- ☐ ....
- ☐ ....
- ☐ ....

Priorities

Enthusiastic for

Appointments

- ☐ ....
- ☐ ....
- ☐ ....
- ☐ ....
- ☐ ....

Breakfast

Lunch

Dinner

Snacks

Fitness

- ☐ ....
- ☐ ....
- ☐ ....

Mood

☺ ☺ ☹

- ☐ ....

DAY PLANNER

Date: ....

To do List

- ☐ ....
- ☐ ....
- ☐ ....
- ☐ ....
- ☐ ....
- ☐ ....
- ☐ ....
- ☐ ....
- ☐ ....
- ☐ ....
- ☐ ....
- ☐ ....
- ☐ ....
- ☐ ....
- ☐ ....
- ☐ ....

Priorities

Enthusiastic for

Appointments

- ☐ ....
- ☐ ....
- ☐ ....
- ☐ ....
- ☐ ....

Breakfast

Lunch

Dinner

Snacks

Fitness

- ☐ ....
- ☐ ....
- ☐ ....

Mood

☺ ☺ ☹

☐ ....

DAY PLANNER

Date: ....

To do List

- ☐ ....
- ☐ ....
- ☐ ....
- ☐ ....
- ☐ ....
- ☐ ....
- ☐ ....
- ☐ ....
- ☐ ....
- ☐ ....
- ☐ ....
- ☐ ....
- ☐ ....
- ☐ ....
- ☐ ....

Priorities

Enthusiastic for

Appointments

- ☐ ....
- ☐ ....
- ☐ ....
- ☐ ....
- ☐ ....

Breakfast

Lunch

Dinner

Snacks

Fitness

- ☐ ....
- ☐ ....
- ☐ ....

Mood

☺ ☺ ☹

- ☐ ....

DAY PLANNER

Date: ....

To do List

- ☐ ....
- ☐ ....
- ☐ ....
- ☐ ....
- ☐ ....
- ☐ ....
- ☐ ....
- ☐ ....
- ☐ ....
- ☐ ....
- ☐ ....
- ☐ ....
- ☐ ....
- ☐ ....
- ☐ ....
- ☐ ....

Priorities

Enthusiastic for

Appointments

- ☐ ....
- ☐ ....
- ☐ ....
- ☐ ....
- ☐ ....

Breakfast

Lunch

Dinner

Snacks

Fitness

- ☐ ....
- ☐ ....
- ☐ ....

Mood

☺ ☻ ☹

☐ ....

DAY PLANNER

Date: ....

To do List

- ☐ ....
- ☐ ....
- ☐ ....
- ☐ ....
- ☐ ....
- ☐ ....
- ☐ ....
- ☐ ....
- ☐ ....
- ☐ ....
- ☐ ....
- ☐ ....
- ☐ ....
- ☐ ....
- ☐ ....

Priorities

Enthusiastic for

Appointments

- ☐ ....
- ☐ ....
- ☐ ....
- ☐ ....
- ☐ ....

Breakfast

Lunch

Dinner

Snacks

Fitness

- ☐ ....
- ☐ ....
- ☐ ....

Mood

☺ ☻ ☹

☐ ....

DAY PLANNER

Date: ....

To do List

- ☐ ....
- ☐ ....
- ☐ ....
- ☐ ....
- ☐ ....
- ☐ ....
- ☐ ....
- ☐ ....
- ☐ ....
- ☐ ....
- ☐ ....
- ☐ ....
- ☐ ....
- ☐ ....
- ☐ ....

Priorities

Enthusiastic for

Appointments

- ☐ ....
- ☐ ....
- ☐ ....
- ☐ ....
- ☐ ....

Breakfast

Lunch

Dinner

Snacks

Fitness

- ☐ ....
- ☐ ....
- ☐ ....

Mood

☺ 😐 ☹

☐ ....

DAY PLANNER

Date: ....

To do List

- ☐ ....
- ☐ ....
- ☐ ....
- ☐ ....
- ☐ ....
- ☐ ....
- ☐ ....
- ☐ ....
- ☐ ....
- ☐ ....
- ☐ ....
- ☐ ....
- ☐ ....
- ☐ ....
- ☐ ....

Priorities

Enthusiastic for

Appointments

- ☐ ....
- ☐ ....
- ☐ ....
- ☐ ....
- ☐ ....

Breakfast

Lunch

Dinner

Snacks

Fitness

- ☐ ....
- ☐ ....
- ☐ ....

Mood

☺ ☺ ☹

- ☐ ....

DAY PLANNER

Date: ....

To do List

- ☐ ....
- ☐ ....
- ☐ ....
- ☐ ....
- ☐ ....
- ☐ ....
- ☐ ....
- ☐ ....
- ☐ ....
- ☐ ....
- ☐ ....
- ☐ ....
- ☐ ....
- ☐ ....
- ☐ ....
- ☐ ....

Priorities

Enthusiastic for

Appointments

- ☐ ....
- ☐ ....
- ☐ ....
- ☐ ....
- ☐ ....

Breakfast

Lunch

Dinner

Snacks

Fitness

- ☐ ....
- ☐ ....
- ☐ ....

Mood

☺ ☺ ☹

☐ ....

DAY PLANNER

Date: ....

To do List

- ☐ ....
- ☐ ....
- ☐ ....
- ☐ ....
- ☐ ....
- ☐ ....
- ☐ ....
- ☐ ....
- ☐ ....
- ☐ ....
- ☐ ....
- ☐ ....
- ☐ ....
- ☐ ....
- ☐ ....
- ☐ ....

Priorities

Enthusiastic for

Appointments

- ☐ ....
- ☐ ....
- ☐ ....
- ☐ ....
- ☐ ....

Breakfast

Lunch

Dinner

Snacks

Fitness

- ☐ ....
- ☐ ....
- ☐ ....

Mood

☺   ☺   ☹

- ☐ ....

DAY PLANNER

Date: ....

To do List

- ☐ ....
- ☐ ....
- ☐ ....
- ☐ ....
- ☐ ....
- ☐ ....
- ☐ ....
- ☐ ....
- ☐ ....
- ☐ ....
- ☐ ....
- ☐ ....
- ☐ ....
- ☐ ....
- ☐ ....
- ☐ ....

Priorities

Enthusiastic for

Appointments

- ☐ ....
- ☐ ....
- ☐ ....
- ☐ ....
- ☐ ....

Breakfast

Lunch

Dinner

Snacks

Fitness

- ☐ ....
- ☐ ....
- ☐ ....

Mood

☺ ☺ ☹

☐ ....

DAY PLANNER

Date: ....

To do List

- ☐ ....
- ☐ ....
- ☐ ....
- ☐ ....
- ☐ ....
- ☐ ....
- ☐ ....
- ☐ ....
- ☐ ....
- ☐ ....
- ☐ ....
- ☐ ....
- ☐ ....
- ☐ ....
- ☐ ....

Priorities

Enthusiastic for

Appointments

- ☐ ....
- ☐ ....
- ☐ ....
- ☐ ....
- ☐ ....

Breakfast

Lunch

Dinner

Snacks

Fitness

- ☐ ....
- ☐ ....
- ☐ ....

Mood

☺   ☻   ☹

☐ ....

DAY PLANNER

Date: ....

To do List

- ☐ ....
- ☐ ....
- ☐ ....
- ☐ ....
- ☐ ....
- ☐ ....
- ☐ ....
- ☐ ....
- ☐ ....
- ☐ ....
- ☐ ....
- ☐ ....
- ☐ ....
- ☐ ....
- ☐ ....

Priorities

Enthusiastic for

Appointments

- ☐ ....
- ☐ ....
- ☐ ....
- ☐ ....
- ☐ ....

Breakfast

Lunch

Dinner

Snacks

Fitness

- ☐ ....
- ☐ ....
- ☐ ....

Mood

☺ ☻ ☹

☐ ....

DAY PLANNER

Date: ....

To do List

- ☐ ....
- ☐ ....
- ☐ ....
- ☐ ....
- ☐ ....
- ☐ ....
- ☐ ....
- ☐ ....
- ☐ ....
- ☐ ....
- ☐ ....
- ☐ ....
- ☐ ....
- ☐ ....
- ☐ ....

Priorities

Enthusiastic for

Appointments

- ☐ ....
- ☐ ....
- ☐ ....
- ☐ ....
- ☐ ....

Breakfast

Lunch

Dinner

Snacks

Fitness

- ☐ ....
- ☐ ....
- ☐ ....

Mood

☺   ☺   ☹

- ☐ ....

DAY PLANNER

Date: ....

To do List

- [ ] ....
- [ ] ....
- [ ] ....
- [ ] ....
- [ ] ....
- [ ] ....
- [ ] ....
- [ ] ....
- [ ] ....
- [ ] ....
- [ ] ....
- [ ] ....
- [ ] ....
- [ ] ....
- [ ] ....
- [ ] ....

Priorities

Enthusiastic for

Appointments

- [ ] ....
- [ ] ....
- [ ] ....
- [ ] ....
- [ ] ....

Breakfast   ## Lunch   ## Dinner   ## Snacks

Fitness

- [ ] ....
- [ ] ....
- [ ] ....

Mood

☺   😐   ☹

- [ ] ....

DAY PLANNER

Date: ....

To do List

- ☐ ....
- ☐ ....
- ☐ ....
- ☐ ....
- ☐ ....
- ☐ ....
- ☐ ....
- ☐ ....
- ☐ ....
- ☐ ....
- ☐ ....
- ☐ ....
- ☐ ....
- ☐ ....
- ☐ ....
- ☐ ....

Priorities

Enthusiastic for

Appointments

- ☐ ....
- ☐ ....
- ☐ ....
- ☐ ....
- ☐ ....

Breakfast

Lunch

Dinner

Snacks

Fitness

- ☐ ....
- ☐ ....
- ☐ ....

Mood

☺   😐   ☹

- ☐ ....

DAY PLANNER

Date: ....

To do List

- ☐ ....
- ☐ ....
- ☐ ....
- ☐ ....
- ☐ ....
- ☐ ....
- ☐ ....
- ☐ ....
- ☐ ....
- ☐ ....
- ☐ ....
- ☐ ....
- ☐ ....
- ☐ ....
- ☐ ....
- ☐ ....

Priorities

Enthusiastic for

Appointments

- ☐ ....
- ☐ ....
- ☐ ....
- ☐ ....
- ☐ ....

Breakfast

Lunch

Dinner

Snacks

Fitness

- ☐ ....
- ☐ ....
- ☐ ....

Mood

☺   😐   ☹

☐ ....

DAY PLANNER

Date: ....

To do List

- ☐ ....
- ☐ ....
- ☐ ....
- ☐ ....
- ☐ ....
- ☐ ....
- ☐ ....
- ☐ ....
- ☐ ....
- ☐ ....
- ☐ ....
- ☐ ....
- ☐ ....
- ☐ ....
- ☐ ....

Priorities

Enthusiastic for

Appointments

- ☐ ....
- ☐ ....
- ☐ ....
- ☐ ....
- ☐ ....

Breakfast

Lunch

Dinner

Snacks

Fitness

- ☐ ....
- ☐ ....
- ☐ ....

Mood

☺ ☐ ☹

- ☐ ....

DAY PLANNER

Date: ....

To do List

- ☐ ....
- ☐ ....
- ☐ ....
- ☐ ....
- ☐ ....
- ☐ ....
- ☐ ....
- ☐ ....
- ☐ ....
- ☐ ....
- ☐ ....
- ☐ ....
- ☐ ....
- ☐ ....
- ☐ ....
- ☐ ....

Priorities

Enthusiastic for

Appointments

- ☐ ....
- ☐ ....
- ☐ ....
- ☐ ....
- ☐ ....

Breakfast

Lunch

Dinner

Snacks

Fitness

- ☐ ....
- ☐ ....
- ☐ ....

Mood

☺ ☻ ☹

☐ ....

DAY PLANNER

Date: ....

To do List

- ☐ ....
- ☐ ....
- ☐ ....
- ☐ ....
- ☐ ....
- ☐ ....
- ☐ ....
- ☐ ....
- ☐ ....
- ☐ ....
- ☐ ....
- ☐ ....
- ☐ ....
- ☐ ....
- ☐ ....
- ☐ ....
- ☐ ....

Priorities

Enthusiastic for

Appointments

- ☐ ....
- ☐ ....
- ☐ ....
- ☐ ....
- ☐ ....

Breakfast

Lunch

Dinner

Snacks

Fitness

- ☐ ....
- ☐ ....
- ☐ ....

Mood

☺ ☹ ☹

☐ ....

DAY PLANNER

Date: ....

To do List

- [ ] ....
- [ ] ....
- [ ] ....
- [ ] ....
- [ ] ....
- [ ] ....
- [ ] ....
- [ ] ....
- [ ] ....
- [ ] ....
- [ ] ....
- [ ] ....
- [ ] ....
- [ ] ....
- [ ] ....

Priorities

Enthusiastic for

Appointments

- [ ] ....
- [ ] ....
- [ ] ....
- [ ] ....
- [ ] ....

Breakfast

Lunch

Dinner

Snacks

Fitness

- [ ] ....
- [ ] ....
- [ ] ....

Mood

☺   😐   ☹

- [ ] ....

DAY PLANNER

Date: ....

To do List

- ☐ ....
- ☐ ....
- ☐ ....
- ☐ ....
- ☐ ....
- ☐ ....
- ☐ ....
- ☐ ....
- ☐ ....
- ☐ ....
- ☐ ....
- ☐ ....
- ☐ ....
- ☐ ....
- ☐ ....
- ☐ ....

Priorities

Enthusiastic for

Appointments

- ☐ ....
- ☐ ....
- ☐ ....
- ☐ ....
- ☐ ....

Breakfast

Lunch

Dinner

Snacks

Fitness

- ☐ ....
- ☐ ....
- ☐ ....

Mood

☺ ☺ ☹

☐ ....

DAY PLANNER

Date: ....

To do List

- ☐ ....
- ☐ ....
- ☐ ....
- ☐ ....
- ☐ ....
- ☐ ....
- ☐ ....
- ☐ ....
- ☐ ....
- ☐ ....
- ☐ ....
- ☐ ....
- ☐ ....
- ☐ ....
- ☐ ....
- ☐ ....

Priorities

Enthusiastic for

Appointments

- ☐ ....
- ☐ ....
- ☐ ....
- ☐ ....
- ☐ ....

Breakfast

Lunch

Dinner

Snacks

Fitness

- ☐ ....
- ☐ ....
- ☐ ....

Mood

☺ ☻ ☹

☐ ....

DAY PLANNER

Date: ....

To do List

- ☐ ....
- ☐ ....
- ☐ ....
- ☐ ....
- ☐ ....
- ☐ ....
- ☐ ....
- ☐ ....
- ☐ ....
- ☐ ....
- ☐ ....
- ☐ ....
- ☐ ....
- ☐ ....
- ☐ ....
- ☐ ....

Priorities

Enthusiastic for

Appointments

- ☐ ....
- ☐ ....
- ☐ ....
- ☐ ....
- ☐ ....

Breakfast

Lunch

Dinner

Snacks

Fitness

- ☐ ....
- ☐ ....
- ☐ ....

Mood

☺   😐   ☹

☐ ....

DAY PLANNER

Date: ....

To do List

- [ ] ....
- [ ] ....
- [ ] ....
- [ ] ....
- [ ] ....
- [ ] ....
- [ ] ....
- [ ] ....
- [ ] ....
- [ ] ....
- [ ] ....
- [ ] ....
- [ ] ....
- [ ] ....
- [ ] ....
- [ ] ....
- [ ] ....

Priorities

Enthusiastic for

Appointments

- [ ] ....
- [ ] ....
- [ ] ....
- [ ] ....
- [ ] ....

Breakfast

Lunch

Dinner

Snacks

Fitness

- [ ] ....
- [ ] ....
- [ ] ....

Mood

☺ 😐 ☹

- [ ] ....

Task List

- [ ]
- [ ]
- [ ]
- [ ]
- [ ]
- [ ]
- [ ]
- [ ]
- [ ]
- [ ]
- [ ]
- [ ]
- [ ]
- [ ]
- [ ]
- [ ]
- [ ]
- [ ]
- [ ]
- [ ]
- [ ]
- [ ]
- [ ]
- [ ]

- [ ]
- [ ]
- [ ]
- [ ]
- [ ]
- [ ]
- [ ]
- [ ]
- [ ]
- [ ]
- [ ]
- [ ]
- [ ]
- [ ]
- [ ]
- [ ]
- [ ]
- [ ]
- [ ]
- [ ]
- [ ]
- [ ]
- [ ]

- [ ]
- [ ]
- [ ]
- [ ]
- [ ]
- [ ]
- [ ]
- [ ]
- [ ]
- [ ]
- [ ]
- [ ]
- [ ]
- [ ]
- [ ]
- [ ]
- [ ]
- [ ]
- [ ]
- [ ]
- [ ]
- [ ]
- [ ]

- [ ]
- [ ]
- [ ]
- [ ]
- [ ]
- [ ]
- [ ]
- [ ]
- [ ]
- [ ]
- [ ]
- [ ]
- [ ]
- [ ]
- [ ]
- [ ]
- [ ]
- [ ]
- [ ]
- [ ]
- [ ]
- [ ]
- [ ]
- [ ]

- [ ]
- [ ]
- [ ]
- [ ]
- [ ]
- [ ]
- [ ]
- [ ]
- [ ]
- [ ]
- [ ]
- [ ]
- [ ]
- [ ]
- [ ]
- [ ]
- [ ]
- [ ]
- [ ]
- [ ]
- [ ]
- [ ]
- [ ]
- [ ]

- [ ]
- [ ]
- [ ]
- [ ]
- [ ]
- [ ]
- [ ]
- [ ]
- [ ]
- [ ]
- [ ]
- [ ]
- [ ]
- [ ]
- [ ]
- [ ]
- [ ]
- [ ]
- [ ]
- [ ]
- [ ]
- [ ]
- [ ]
- [ ]

- [ ]
- [ ]
- [ ]
- [ ]
- [ ]
- [ ]
- [ ]
- [ ]
- [ ]
- [ ]
- [ ]
- [ ]
- [ ]
- [ ]
- [ ]
- [ ]
- [ ]
- [ ]
- [ ]
- [ ]
- [ ]
- [ ]
- [ ]
- [ ]

- [ ]
- [ ]
- [ ]
- [ ]
- [ ]
- [ ]
- [ ]
- [ ]
- [ ]
- [ ]
- [ ]
- [ ]
- [ ]
- [ ]
- [ ]
- [ ]
- [ ]
- [ ]
- [ ]
- [ ]
- [ ]
- [ ]
- [ ]
- [ ]

- [ ]
- [ ]
- [ ]
- [ ]
- [ ]
- [ ]
- [ ]
- [ ]
- [ ]
- [ ]
- [ ]
- [ ]
- [ ]
- [ ]
- [ ]
- [ ]
- [ ]
- [ ]
- [ ]
- [ ]
- [ ]
- [ ]
- [ ]
- [ ]

- [ ]
- [ ]
- [ ]
- [ ]
- [ ]
- [ ]
- [ ]
- [ ]
- [ ]
- [ ]
- [ ]
- [ ]
- [ ]
- [ ]
- [ ]
- [ ]
- [ ]
- [ ]
- [ ]
- [ ]
- [ ]
- [ ]
- [ ]
- [ ]

- [ ]
- [ ]
- [ ]
- [ ]
- [ ]
- [ ]
- [ ]
- [ ]
- [ ]
- [ ]
- [ ]
- [ ]
- [ ]
- [ ]
- [ ]
- [ ]
- [ ]
- [ ]
- [ ]
- [ ]
- [ ]
- [ ]
- [ ]

- [ ]
- [ ]
- [ ]
- [ ]
- [ ]
- [ ]
- [ ]
- [ ]
- [ ]
- [ ]
- [ ]
- [ ]
- [ ]
- [ ]
- [ ]
- [ ]
- [ ]
- [ ]
- [ ]
- [ ]
- [ ]
- [ ]
- [ ]
- [ ]
- [ ]

- [ ]
- [ ]
- [ ]
- [ ]
- [ ]
- [ ]
- [ ]
- [ ]
- [ ]
- [ ]
- [ ]
- [ ]
- [ ]
- [ ]
- [ ]
- [ ]
- [ ]
- [ ]
- [ ]
- [ ]
- [ ]
- [ ]
- [ ]
- [ ]

- [ ]
- [ ]
- [ ]
- [ ]
- [ ]
- [ ]
- [ ]
- [ ]
- [ ]
- [ ]
- [ ]
- [ ]
- [ ]
- [ ]
- [ ]
- [ ]
- [ ]
- [ ]
- [ ]
- [ ]
- [ ]
- [ ]
- [ ]
- [ ]

- [ ]
- [ ]
- [ ]
- [ ]
- [ ]
- [ ]
- [ ]
- [ ]
- [ ]
- [ ]
- [ ]
- [ ]
- [ ]
- [ ]
- [ ]
- [ ]
- [ ]
- [ ]
- [ ]
- [ ]
- [ ]
- [ ]
- [ ]
- [ ]

- [ ]
- [ ]
- [ ]
- [ ]
- [ ]
- [ ]
- [ ]
- [ ]
- [ ]
- [ ]
- [ ]
- [ ]
- [ ]
- [ ]
- [ ]
- [ ]
- [ ]
- [ ]
- [ ]
- [ ]
- [ ]
- [ ]
- [ ]
- [ ]
- [ ]

- [ ]
- [ ]
- [ ]
- [ ]
- [ ]
- [ ]
- [ ]
- [ ]
- [ ]
- [ ]
- [ ]
- [ ]
- [ ]
- [ ]
- [ ]
- [ ]
- [ ]
- [ ]
- [ ]
- [ ]
- [ ]
- [ ]
- [ ]
- [ ]

- [ ]
- [ ]
- [ ]
- [ ]
- [ ]
- [ ]
- [ ]
- [ ]
- [ ]
- [ ]
- [ ]
- [ ]
- [ ]
- [ ]
- [ ]
- [ ]
- [ ]
- [ ]
- [ ]
- [ ]
- [ ]
- [ ]
- [ ]
- [ ]

- [ ]
- [ ]
- [ ]
- [ ]
- [ ]
- [ ]
- [ ]
- [ ]
- [ ]
- [ ]
- [ ]
- [ ]
- [ ]
- [ ]
- [ ]
- [ ]
- [ ]
- [ ]
- [ ]
- [ ]
- [ ]
- [ ]
- [ ]
- [ ]
- [ ]

- [ ]
- [ ]
- [ ]
- [ ]
- [ ]
- [ ]
- [ ]
- [ ]
- [ ]
- [ ]
- [ ]
- [ ]
- [ ]
- [ ]
- [ ]
- [ ]
- [ ]
- [ ]
- [ ]
- [ ]
- [ ]
- [ ]
- [ ]
- [ ]

- [ ]
- [ ]
- [ ]
- [ ]
- [ ]
- [ ]
- [ ]
- [ ]
- [ ]
- [ ]
- [ ]
- [ ]
- [ ]
- [ ]
- [ ]
- [ ]
- [ ]
- [ ]
- [ ]
- [ ]
- [ ]
- [ ]
- [ ]
- [ ]

- [ ]
- [ ]
- [ ]
- [ ]
- [ ]
- [ ]
- [ ]
- [ ]
- [ ]
- [ ]
- [ ]
- [ ]
- [ ]
- [ ]
- [ ]
- [ ]
- [ ]
- [ ]
- [ ]
- [ ]
- [ ]
- [ ]
- [ ]

- [ ]
- [ ]
- [ ]
- [ ]
- [ ]
- [ ]
- [ ]
- [ ]
- [ ]
- [ ]
- [ ]
- [ ]
- [ ]
- [ ]
- [ ]
- [ ]
- [ ]
- [ ]
- [ ]
- [ ]
- [ ]
- [ ]
- [ ]
- [ ]

- [ ]
- [ ]
- [ ]
- [ ]
- [ ]
- [ ]
- [ ]
- [ ]
- [ ]
- [ ]
- [ ]
- [ ]
- [ ]
- [ ]
- [ ]
- [ ]
- [ ]
- [ ]
- [ ]
- [ ]
- [ ]
- [ ]
- [ ]

- [ ]
- [ ]
- [ ]
- [ ]
- [ ]
- [ ]
- [ ]
- [ ]
- [ ]
- [ ]
- [ ]
- [ ]
- [ ]
- [ ]
- [ ]
- [ ]
- [ ]
- [ ]
- [ ]
- [ ]
- [ ]
- [ ]
- [ ]
- [ ]

- [ ]
- [ ]
- [ ]
- [ ]
- [ ]
- [ ]
- [ ]
- [ ]
- [ ]
- [ ]
- [ ]
- [ ]
- [ ]
- [ ]
- [ ]
- [ ]
- [ ]
- [ ]
- [ ]
- [ ]
- [ ]
- [ ]
- [ ]
- [ ]

- [ ]
- [ ]
- [ ]
- [ ]
- [ ]
- [ ]
- [ ]
- [ ]
- [ ]
- [ ]
- [ ]
- [ ]
- [ ]
- [ ]
- [ ]
- [ ]
- [ ]
- [ ]
- [ ]
- [ ]
- [ ]
- [ ]
- [ ]
- [ ]

- [ ]
- [ ]
- [ ]
- [ ]
- [ ]
- [ ]
- [ ]
- [ ]
- [ ]
- [ ]
- [ ]
- [ ]
- [ ]
- [ ]
- [ ]
- [ ]
- [ ]
- [ ]
- [ ]
- [ ]
- [ ]
- [ ]
- [ ]

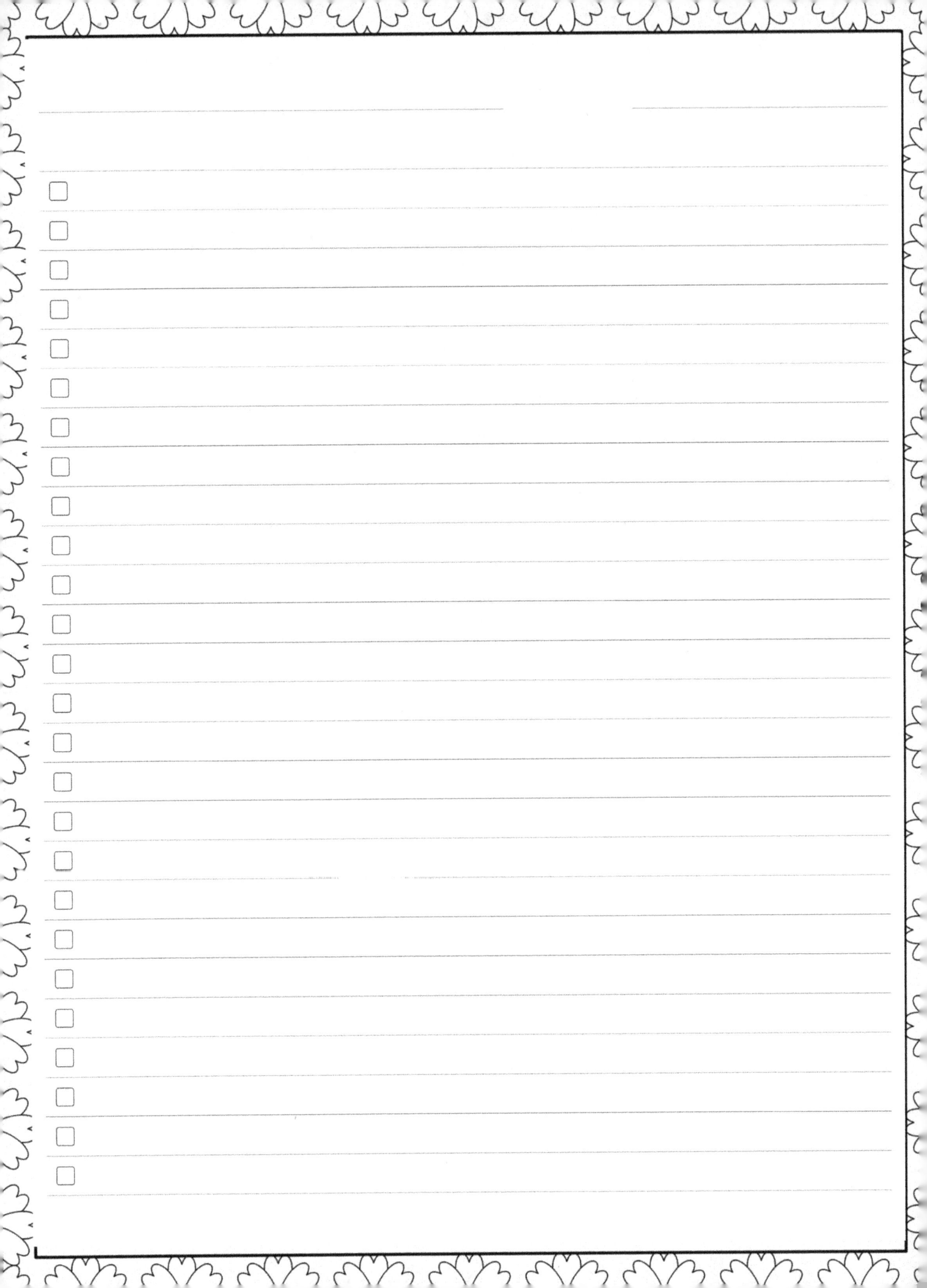

- [ ]
- [ ]
- [ ]
- [ ]
- [ ]
- [ ]
- [ ]
- [ ]
- [ ]
- [ ]
- [ ]
- [ ]
- [ ]
- [ ]
- [ ]
- [ ]
- [ ]
- [ ]
- [ ]
- [ ]
- [ ]
- [ ]
- [ ]
- [ ]

- [ ]
- [ ]
- [ ]
- [ ]
- [ ]
- [ ]
- [ ]
- [ ]
- [ ]
- [ ]
- [ ]
- [ ]
- [ ]
- [ ]
- [ ]
- [ ]
- [ ]
- [ ]
- [ ]
- [ ]
- [ ]
- [ ]
- [ ]
- [ ]

- [ ]
- [ ]
- [ ]
- [ ]
- [ ]
- [ ]
- [ ]
- [ ]
- [ ]
- [ ]
- [ ]
- [ ]
- [ ]
- [ ]
- [ ]
- [ ]
- [ ]
- [ ]
- [ ]
- [ ]
- [ ]
- [ ]
- [ ]

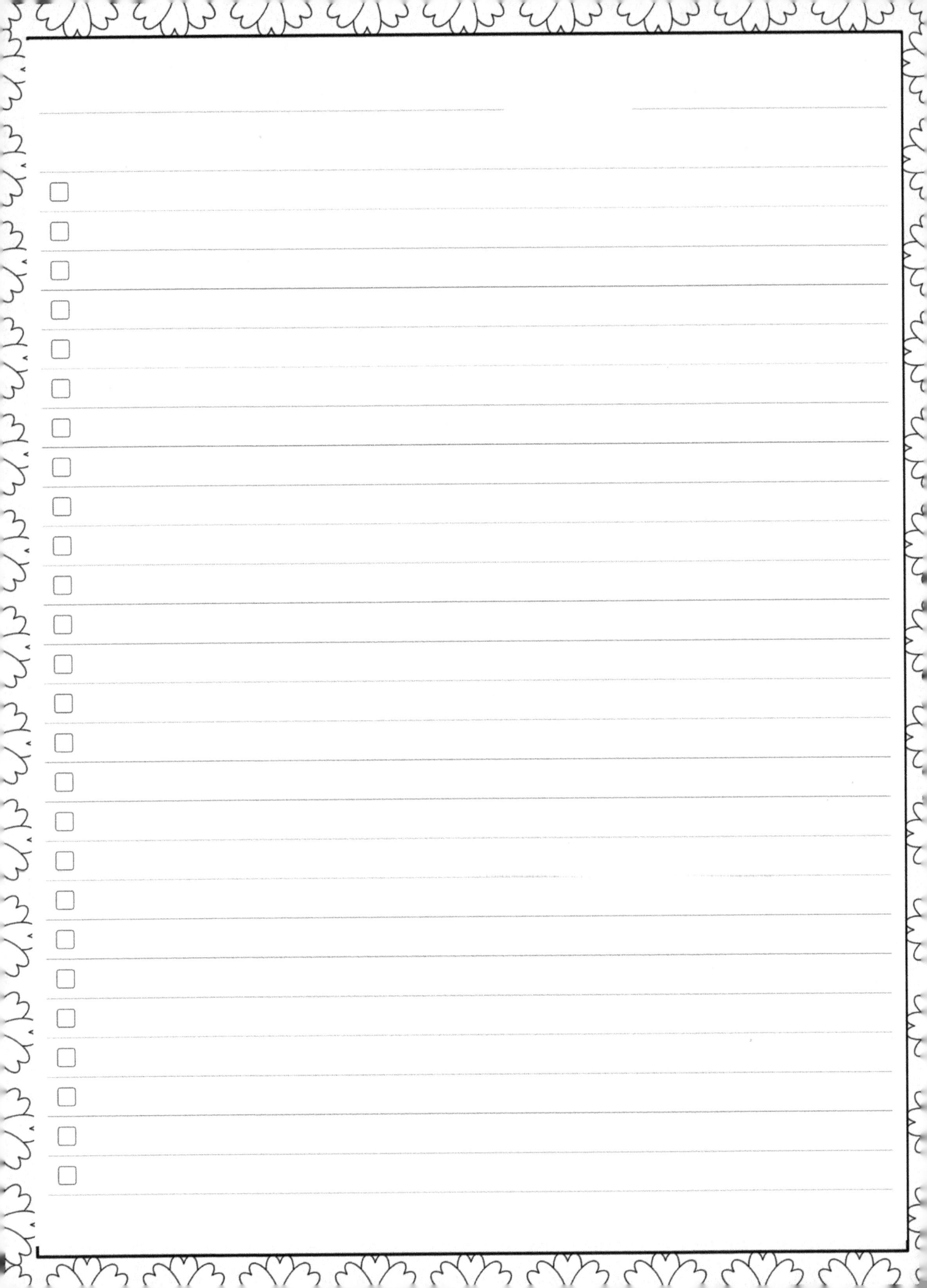

- [ ]
- [ ]
- [ ]
- [ ]
- [ ]
- [ ]
- [ ]
- [ ]
- [ ]
- [ ]
- [ ]
- [ ]
- [ ]
- [ ]
- [ ]
- [ ]
- [ ]
- [ ]
- [ ]
- [ ]
- [ ]
- [ ]
- [ ]
- [ ]
- [ ]

www.ingramcontent.com/pod-product-compliance
Lightning Source LLC
Chambersburg PA
CBHW080549030426

42337CB00024B/4814